Surviving Abuse
Four True Stories

Beth Johnson

TP THE TOWNSEND LIBRARY

Surviving Abuse:
Four True Stories

TP THE TOWNSEND LIBRARY

For more titles in the Townsend Library,
visit our website: **www.townsendpress.com**

Photography:
Kenyon Whittington and Dawn Cogliser by Beth Johnson
Ryan Klootwyk by Nick Tremmel
Eunice Ruiz by Michelle Duesman

ISBN 13: 978-1-59194-057-9
ISBN 10: 1-59194-057-5

Library of Congress Control Number:
2005933215

Contents

Abuse takes many forms, all of them ugly.

● As a small child, Kenyon was beaten and humiliated—first by his mother, later by his father and stepmother.

● At first Dawn's husband called her fat and ugly and said no one else would ever want her. Later he began hitting her.

● Ryan's stepfather kicked and hit him as well as his brother and mother.

● Family gatherings became a nightmare for Eunice when an adult relative began molesting her.

The four people profiled in this book are dissimilar in many ways. When they were being abused, Kenyon was a little boy. Dawn was an adult woman. Ryan was an adolescent. Eunice was only eight. They were separated geographically: Kenyon's abuse occurred in Maryland and Delaware. Dawn was living in Pennsylvania. Ryan was moving all over the country, and Eunice lived in Mexico.

But certain things bind all four of these people's experiences together. The same things could be said of almost any victim of abuse.

● Each of them felt *powerless* to stand up to his or her abuser. They saw their abusers as bigger, more powerful, and more important than they were. It seemed to them at the time that their abusers held all the cards, and that they had to take what the abusers dished out.

● Each of them felt somehow *responsible* for the abuse. In their minds, the abuse happened at least in part because they were doing something wrong. They came to believe that if only they were smarter, or quicker, or better, or prettier, or braver, they would not be targeted for abuse.

● Each of them remained *silent* about the abuse for a long time. They didn't tell what was happening for a variety of reasons. Kenyon was too young to ask for help. Dawn was ashamed and wanted to believe her husband's promises to change. Ryan feared that asking for help would further endanger his mother. Eunice thought she would not be believed, or that if she was believed that she would be blamed.

Finally, however, all four of these people did speak out about what had happened to them. Although they still bear emotional as well as physical scars from their abuse, they have moved on and are living whole, happy, productive lives. As Eunice Ruiz puts it, "Being molested is something that happened to me. It does not define who I am."

Tragically, many victims of abuse have not taken the positive steps that Kenyon, Dawn, Ryan, and Eunice have. Weighed down by fear, guilt, depression and confusion, they continue to live in abusive situations today.

Because there is so much secrecy involved in domestic abuse, it's hard to be sure exactly how common it is. But here are a few statistics that reflect what we do know:

● Domestic violence is the #1 cause for women to visit emergency rooms.

● Seventy percent of men who batter their wives or girlfriends also beat or molest their children.

● One in four girls and one in seven boys is molested during childhood.

It's upsetting to know that domestic abuse is so common. But that knowledge could actually be comforting to someone who is being victimized. Victims of abuse usually feel very alone. They often believe that no one could understand what they're going through. They think there must be something very unusual and wrong about them to be in such a position. But the fact is, many hundreds of thousands of people have lived—or are now living—in similar situations.

The stories of Kenyon, Dawn, Ryan, and Eunice show that abuse can take many forms, not all of them easy to detect. Spousal abuse can be especially hard to identify, even by the adult who is being abused. To help clarify what abuse of a partner actually is, here is a list of questions to consider. People who answer "Yes" to any of these questions should consider the possibility that they are in an abusive relationship . . .

Does your partner frequently tell you that you are stupid and everything wrong with the relationship is your fault?

Does your partner tell you that no one else will ever want you?

Does your partner control which friends or relatives you can see or talk to?

Does your partner control how and when you use the phone?

Does your partner threaten to hurt himself/herself, your children, or your pets if you leave him/her?

Does your partner force you to have sex?

Does your partner demand that you account for every minute you are out of his/her sight?

Does your partner ever lock you in or out of your home?

Does your partner prevent you from going to school or getting a job?

Does your partner take your money?

Do you keep trying to please your partner in the hope that he/she will change?

Does your partner hit, slap, kick, or push you?

What if a person is being abused? What steps can he or she take?

If the person is an adult, here are some steps she or he might consider:

● **Reach out**. As a victim of abuse, you are probably feeling very alone. Your abuser is counting on this isolation to keep you quiet and controllable. One of the most effective things you can do is reach out for support from family, friends, co-workers, church members, social service agencies, and hotline volunteers. The National Domestic Violence Hotline is 1-800-799-SAFE (7233). Merely talking to people about what's happening will be a big step toward dealing with it.

● **Develop a safety plan.** Look ahead and decide what you will do if you reach the point that you choose to leave. Have an "escape bag" ready and hidden somewhere safe. That bag should include an extra set of car keys, identification documents, insurance cards, medications you need, some cash, etc.

Determine where you would be able to go if you left. Your destination might be a friend's house or a shelter. The important thing is that you have a place in mind and know how to get there.

● If you have children, talk to a lawyer (call your local Legal Aid office for low-cost help) before you leave so that you know how to protect your custody rights.

● Remember: IT IS NOT YOUR FAULT YOU ARE BEING ABUSED. Your abuser may blame you for "making" him/her angry and abusive. This is a lie. No one "makes" another person become abusive. The abuser is the one responsible for the abuse, not the victim.

What if you are a minor who is being abused?

● Remember that there are very strong laws to protect children from abuse. But those laws can only help if you let people know what's happening to you.

● Get the help of as many people as you can. Tell a trusted teacher or coach or guidance counselor at school. Call your local child protective service agency. Or call the National Child Abuse Hotline at

1-800-4-A-Child (1-800-422-4453). Report your situation to a police officer. All these people are required by law to investigate your report.

Whether you yourself are a victim of abuse, or whether you are concerned about someone who may be being abused, remember this: Abuse is a practice that thrives on secrecy and shame. Whatever any of us can do to pull it into the bright light of day, look directly at it and talk about it openly will lessen its power.

The only one who should feel ashamed about abuse is an abuser.

There is no excuse for abuse.

If you see abuse, tell someone.

Kenyon

Kenyon Whittington

Child-development experts often say that the first few years of a child's life are the most important. They warn that if a child does not receive plenty of love and positive stimulation during those earliest years, the child's social and intellectual development may never catch up.

If they are right, it's hard to explain Kenyon Whittington. Kenyon came into the world under circumstances that could hardly have been less promising. When his mother, Angie*, became pregnant, she and her boyfriend Lamar* were both annoyed. They already had a five-year-old daughter, and they did not want another child. Family members did not even learn of the pregnancy until shortly before the baby arrived.

*Not their real names

When Kenyon's paternal aunt, Fay, went to visit mom and baby in the hospital, she was disturbed by what she found there.

"He came into the world just like the baby Jesus, with nothing but what he brought with him," she remembers. "The hospital had to provide a little outfit and blanket for him."

The baby didn't even have a name. Fay asked if his mother wanted to name him Lamar, after his father. "Hell, no," Angie said. "You can name him." The television was on in the hospital room, and as the credits for a show were rolling, Fay noticed the name "Kenyon" flash by. She took the unusual name as a sign from God, and suggested the baby be called that. Angie agreed.

"You can have him," Angie told Fay.

"I laughed," Fay says. "I thought she was joking."

Nevertheless, when Fay drove the baby and his mother home from the hospital, Angie got out of the car, walked down the avenue, and vanished. Fay was left staring at the baby nephew in her arms.

Fay, who was single, was a teacher at a Philadelphia elementary school. She shared a home in Johnson Holmes Projects with her mother, Ruth. Suddenly responsible for a newborn child, she called her employer, arranged to take a half-day off, and headed home.

"Thank the Lord my mother was there," she says. "I just walked in and said, 'Mom, the baby's here.' There was never any question that we'd keep him."

Kenyon's father, Lamar, was living in the household at the time as well, but he took little interest in the child. "If the baby was beside him on the couch, I guess he'd keep him from rolling off, but that's about it," Fay says. "If Mother and I left for a few hours and came back, it was clear he hadn't changed his diaper or washed him or anything. Maybe he would give him a bottle, but I am not entirely sure he'd do even that. His son meant nothing to him."

Lamar's neglect of the baby disgusted his sister. Lamar was a highly intelligent man, a prolific writer, and a creative artist. He was also a college graduate who, at the time, worked as a substitute teacher. But perhaps because his relationship with Angie was failing, he never seemed to connect to the baby. It angered Fay that he did not take more of an interest, and the brother and sister's relationship suffered. "We'd been close as could be when we were younger," Fay says, but now resentment grew between the two.

As Kenyon grew into a toddler, Angie showed an occasional interest in her son, sometimes taking him to stay with her at the house she shared with her sister and brother in Maryland. Perhaps because of the trauma of being abandoned by his parents, Kenyon was late in learning to talk. He could not tell Fay and his grandmother what life at his mother's house was like. Nevertheless, he remembers it vividly.

Kenyon at age five

"I'd sit on the couch, real quiet, trying not to set her off," he says. "I never knew what it was that made her so angry. But suddenly she would just snatch me and start slapping and beating on me, sometimes whipping me with a large black belt.

"My aunt Faustine would try to stop her, saying, 'Angie, leave the boy alone!' But that would make my mother all the angrier. Sometimes my uncle would beat down my mother for mistreating me. She'd tell both my uncle and Faustine it was none of their business, and that she could do anything she wanted with me. She'd beat me and then leave me in her dark bedroom. Sometimes I saw things move in the darkness. I was alone and terrified."

One evening when Kenyon was four, the abuse reached a new level. Angie became nearly hysterical, "screaming, cursing, and hitting me," Kenyon recalls. "I ran to Aunt Faustine, but my mother caught me and dragged me into the bedroom and began beating me, pounding me down to the floor." Afraid for Kenyon's life, Faustine called the police.

Kenyon remembers the hours that followed as a puzzled blur of images. "State troopers came. They were the first Caucasian people I'd ever seen," he says. "I remember one female trooper talking to me in a very polite tone. As she continued to talk to me, I began to feel a sense of protection. They took me out of there and to the police station. It was cold, and one of the officers brought me a warm blanket."

At the station, the troopers saw the bruises from the beating Kenyon had received. They assured Kenyon they would not return him to his mother. But as they looked into the little boy's case, they discovered an unfortunate fact: even though Kenyon rarely lived with his mother, she still had legal custody of her son. As far as the authorities were concerned, Fay and

Kenyon and his Aunt Fay look through a collection
of family photos.

Ruth were merely relatives who had no special claim
on the boy. Moreover, Fay and Ruth did not even
know that the boy had been removed from Angie's
home—they assumed he was staying with his mother
longer than usual. So rather than being returned to
his aunt and grandmother, Kenyon was made a ward
of the court. In the meantime, Angie fled to Florida.

For the next half-year, Kenyon drifted from foster home to foster home. "I stayed with a lot of families and met a lot of kids in situations like mine," he says. "It was a rootless and scary way to live. At one point, I lived with my mother's mother. She didn't beat me, but she horrified me. I shared a bed with her, and she slept with a huge butcher knife under her pillow. She'd tell me that if I moved too much during the night, she'd cut my head off."

Finally, the state contacted Kenyon's relatives—including his father, Fay, and Ruth—and brought them together for a meeting to decide where Kenyon should go. Fay was horrified to learn that Kenyon had been in the foster care system all that time. She believed he had been with his mother. She and Ruth were eager to take him home with them again, but his father objected. He was married by then. Kenyon's sister, Yolanda, lived with him and his wife, as did their baby girl (Kenyon's half-sister) and his wife's daughter by a previous relationship. He said he wanted the boy to move in with them as well.

Fay was surprised. "I remember saying, 'Are you sure, Lamar?'" she says. But Lamar insisted he was. As Kenyon's father, Lamar had the strongest natural claim to the boy, and the court was glad to hand him over. Fay and Ruth tried to be glad, too. "We wanted to believe this was a good thing," Fay says. "We wanted to think, well, Lamar is his father and he's come around to wanting to do right by him."

Tragically, that was not the case. Lamar and his wife quickly began abusing Kenyon even more severely than his mother ever had. They punished him viciously for the slightest misbehavior, such as his refusal to eat peas.

"I didn't like peas. I couldn't make myself swallow them," Kenyon remembers. "So to punish me for not eating them, they'd hit me, then make me stand in the corner of their dark bedroom. I would stand there for hours. Actually, that is how I learned my numbers. The only thing I could see in the dark was the red-lighted numbers of the digital clock. I'd watch them as they changed: 7. 4. 5. I'd say them to myself. Sometimes during the evening, they'd walk in there to get something. They'd get it and leave, completely ignoring me. It was as if I didn't exist."

Eventually Kenyon would need to use the bathroom. "I'd call to them, asking if I could leave the room. They would always respond 'no.' Finally I would urinate on myself."

Then the most shameful abuse of all would occur. "They'd walk in and say, 'What's that smell? Did you pee on yourself?' Then they would beat me for wetting my clothes." His father would hold him while his stepmother whipped him with the wet garments, even wringing drops of urine onto his face. Humiliated, Kenyon would try to fight and run; frustrated at his resistance, they would separately tie his hands and feet together and gag him by putting one sock in his mouth and tying another one around his eyes. "To this day, I cannot stand the sight of those long white

Kenyon and Fay stand outside Kenyon's apartment in Philadelphia.

tube socks with the stripe around the top," Kenyon says. Finally they would put Kenyon in a bathtub full of cold water with the shower spraying.

"When they were done, they'd say, 'Have you learned your lesson yet?' Then they'd send me to bed."

"Bed" was the floor of the bedroom he shared with his little half-sister. She slept in her crib. "I would lie there watching her sleep and wonder why I was the only one to receive beatings. Why was I the

Kenyon's grandmother, Ruth, was the woman Kenyon called "Mom."

unwanted one?" Not only was Kenyon the only child in the house to be abused, but he was isolated almost constantly from his sisters. They spent much of their time in the living room, where the television was.

In the year that Kenyon lived with his father, he remembers being in that room once. "I basically lived in the corner of my father's bedroom."

During the year, Kenyon visited his grandmother and Fay only one time. He was still a silent child, and in his father's presence, he said nothing about how he was being treated. However, he did say one thing that haunted Fay.

"He looked at me, this little child, and asked, 'Are you happy?'" Fay shook her head at the memory.

"'Are you happy?' from a four- or five-year-old! That struck me as so strange, so troubling."

Perhaps Fay was still thinking of that question when, soon after, she had a disturbing dream. In it, she saw Kenyon and Yolanda at the bottom of a dark pit. She saw Kenyon reaching out to her, saying, "Help me."

"I'm afraid for the children," she told her mother.

"I said, 'Mother, we have to go to court and get legal custody.' I just knew somehow it was time to play hardball."

Once informed that Fay and Ruth were seeking legal custody, Lamar quickly agreed to let the children go. Soon, Kenyon was back with his aunt and grandmother—for good, this time.

Fay and Ruth were happy and relieved to have the children back. "We had a party, with balloons and a cake and all," Fay remembers. "It wasn't anyone's birthday; it was just to celebrate that they were here, and that we wouldn't be separated again."

As their life together began, Fay noticed a few unusual things about Kenyon: for example, he and Yolanda were both unnaturally quiet.

"In the classroom, I was always having to hush children and ask them to not be so noisy," she remembers. "But with these two, I began to hope for some ordinary yelling and running around. Sometimes I'd hear them talking quietly, but as soon as any adult or I came near, they were silent as they could be. In addition, Kenyon would sit on the couch so quietly, with his feet crossed and his hands clasped on his lap. It was not natural. It was clear that he was afraid just to act like a little boy."

But gradually, Fay and Ruth learned the details of how Kenyon had been treated. Even then, Fay did not want to believe that her brother could have been so cruel to his son. "Kenyon would show me how he was gagged—how his tongue was pushed back in his mouth from the sock being shoved in there," says Fay, tears welling in her eyes at the memory. "I'd say,

As an adult, Kenyon never forgets all his Aunt Fay and his late
grandmother did to help him.

'But Kenyon—your *father* didn't do that to you.' And he would say, 'He was there. He held me down.'"

Such knowledge embittered Fay deeply. "If the courts hadn't given them to us—well, I would be ashamed to tell you some of the things I thought of during that time," Fay says. "I actually thought about kidnapping them. And if my brother had put up a fight over handing them over, I would have been willing to take his life."

One of the unanswered questions of Kenyon's life is why his father had taken him in the first place, when he knew that Fay and Ruth loved him and would have gladly given him a home. Fay shakes her head bitterly at the question. "I can only think it was to spite me," she says. "He resented me being like a mother to Kenyon, so he did it to show me that he could."

Her theory is supported by something that Kenyon remembers. "When I was with my father, the worst thing I could do was to ask for Aunt Fay," he says. "That made him terribly angry. Once when I said I wanted her, they threw me out into the snow."

In addition, Fay says, her own father was physically and mentally abusive. "I'm a verbal person, and I think I've been able to talk out how I felt about what happened to us," she says. "But Lamar was quiet. Maybe the abuse he experienced just stayed within him in a way that poisoned him. And I can understand and sympathize with that—to a point. But not to the point that he'd hurt another child."

With the resilience of a child, Kenyon began to regain his happiness and confidence. His life with his aunt and grandmother (whom he soon began calling Mom) was peaceful and positive.

After all these years, Kenyon's voice still grows hushed and wondering as he speaks of Fay and Ruth. "Those women—they are *diamonds*. They mean the world to me," he says. "They saved me. They just flat-out saved me."

"They were strong people," he continued. "They

Kenyon relaxes at home by playing the guitar.

had very strong beliefs, very strong values. Be upright. Tell the truth. Go to church. Value education. Be moral, be responsible. And if you didn't uphold those values," Kenyon says with a grin, "you got your butt kicked."

"Butt kicking" was a very different matter than the abuse he had suffered at the hands of his parents. "Yes, they were old-fashioned women who used physical punishment," Kenyon explains. "But they punished me with love, in order to chasten me. They never went over the line into abuse. They would talk to me first, tell me what I had done and why they were punishing me. They were teaching me to think about consequences, that sometimes you don't get a second chance to do the right thing. I understood that logic.

"When my birth parents beat me, it was simply to destroy me. With them, I knew all hope was lost. When Mom and Aunt Fay punished me, I felt respected and loved."

But most of Kenyon's time with his grandmother and aunt was not about punishment, but about love and learning. "Aunt Fay bought me those little magnetic letters that you can stick on the refrigerator," he remembers fondly. "She began to teach me to spell words, starting with my name." Kenyon noticed that his grandmother was constantly reading—usually the Bible, but also novels of all kinds. At bedtime, she and Fay would read stories to him. Eager to imitate his elders, Kenyon began reading himself. *The Cat in the Hat* and other Dr. Seuss books were his earliest favorites. Later, Fay introduced him to favorite authors such as Naim Akbar, who writes about psychology and the African-American community.

As he began elementary school, Kenyon established two reputations for himself—as a smart little boy and as a fighter. "It was a tough area we lived in, and I thought I *had* to fight," he explains. "Mom had to go into the school again and again because I was in trouble." Eventually his grandmother had a talk with Kenyon, explaining how hard it was on her to see him in trouble when she was trying so hard to

During a summer of being grounded after sixth grade, Kenyon
developed the lifelong habit of reading.

show him the right way. "Her tears sank in," Kenyon remembers. "The last thing I wanted to do was hurt her." He began to avoid fights and apply himself to his schoolwork. His progress was so rapid that he was invited to participate in a citywide program for gifted students. "I did well," he says. "My anger died down. I began to feel that I was somebody special."

Kenyon continued to do well in school, with a brief detour in sixth grade. He and his grandmother moved to Crisfield, Maryland, with Aunt Fay staying behind in Philadelphia. Upset that he would see less of his aunt, he temporarily lost his focus. His grades plummeted so badly that he was forced to repeat sixth grade.

"My aunt was so fed up with me!" he remembers. "But my grandmother never lost faith. She kept saying, 'It's a phase. He'll come out of it.'" But just to help Kenyon get past his "phase," he was grounded for the entire summer following sixth grade.

"All my entertainment was taken away. There was

no TV, no movies, no phone, and no radio. Just my room, my books, and me. And when you're alone in your room with nothing to do but read..." he says with a chuckle, "well, you read quite a lot." As unhappy as Kenyon was about his "punishment summer," he appreciates the effect it had on him. "I became more of a reader that summer than I'd ever been before."

His sixth-grade experience had taught him something else. "I realized that by trying to fit in with the 'cool' crowd, I was actually going against my nature," Kenyon says. "I saw that their coolness wasn't going to carry them very far in life. I stopped trying to be 'in' and started applying myself. I sought out worthwhile friends. I went to church. I kept reading. I got involved in creating my own life."

As part of that effort, Kenyon joined Project Challenge, an organization that matched African-American men with boys who needed their leadership. These adult mentors spent time with

At home, Kenyon catches up on some work for his job as a
coordinator of the Pennsylvania GEAR UP organization.

Kenyon, taking him out to dinner and movies, helping him look ahead to college, and more important,
just talking to him about life. "That program was
extremely important to me," he notes. "As much as
Aunt Fay and my grandmother did, they couldn't
provide that consistent, positive male presence in my
life. Without a father around, I needed that badly."

Kenyon's beloved grandmother died when he

was fourteen, and after that, he made his home with Aunt Fay in Philadelphia. As Fay works to earn her own doctoral degree, she has encouraged Kenyon to pursue his educational goals. He has taken her encouragement to heart. In high school, he became involved in student government, eventually serving as student council president as well as captain of the debate team and chess team. He also became involved in several enrichment programs, such as the University of Pennsylvania Upward Bound Program and Philadelphia Futures. As part of an organization called Operation Understanding, he visited West Africa and Israel.

After finishing high school, Kenyon attended Hampton University in Virginia. While his family life had become more stable, it was still far from average: to arrive at college, he took an eight-hour Greyhound bus trip alone, and then watched other students arriving with their parents while he unpacked his suitcases alone. He shrugs off the pangs that he felt as such moments. "Such things have taught me to be strong, to rely on myself." He graduated with a degree in political science.

Today Kenyon is a direct services coordinator for the Pennsylvania GEAR UP (Gaining Early Awareness and Readiness for Undergraduate Programs) organization. Through GEAR UP, he helps steer middle- and high school students toward college.

He has now begun working on a master's degree in education with the thought of teaching at the elementary level, but the most important consideration in his future is the well-being of the family he hopes to someday have. Perhaps his own unhappy experience as a child is in his mind when he says, "My first priority is to achieve a happy, healthy family. I want to be an excellent husband and father and a good provider for my children. I see so many men who don't do that, and I will not be like them."

He looks back on his difficult childhood without self-pity, but with the knowledge that he will probably

Kenyon is now studying for his master's degree in education.

never know why things happened as they did.

"I've never hated my parents," he says. "My grand-mother always taught me that despite everything, they were my parents, and that I needed to honor them. That does not mean that I have to associate with them, but I do not curse them, either. She would say, 'God knows what they did, and you know. That's enough.'"

He acknowledges, though, that the memories still hurt. "As an adult, I sometimes see friends with their parents, and it hits me, you know that there is supposed to be a bond there that just never existed for me. I know many people who have had bad relationships with one parent, but it is as if I got the double whammy, with both of them abusing me.

"I hung on to some hopes for a long time," he adds. "When I graduated from high school, I thought maybe they'd show up. And at college graduation, that thought crossed my mind again. I've sometimes thought, 'Maybe they'll learn about the good things I've done and want to acknowledge that I'm their son.'"

Aunt Fay, who was listening to Kenyon, broke in. "But Kenyon—they *know* the good things. At least your dad does." She reminded Kenyon that Lamar talks with friends and family members occasionally. Although he never asks about Kenyon, people volunteer news about the accomplished young man. As for Kenyon's mother, her mental health has worsened to the point that relatives compare her to a young child.

Kenyon nods. He is realistic enough to know that his parents are not likely to ever play a role in his life. A kind and compassionate young man, he speaks of them in a way that would make his grandmother proud.

"You know, I feel sorry for them," he concludes. "They've missed a lot."

Dawn

Dawn Cogliser

*D*awn Cogliser's home is the definition of "warm and cozy." The living room walls are a cheerful purple; the hallway is a deep burnt orange. An enormous soft chair is just the right size for an adult and child to snuggle in together. Children's artwork covers the walls; colorful balloons, left over from the previous day's birthday party, dangle everywhere. A friendly cat and a St. Bernard puppy wander through the house.

Dawn herself sits in a comfortable rocking chair. When her husband and three children come in the door, the kids pile on top of her as if she were a sofa.

Dawn hoists eighteen-month-old Zane high in the air. "Ooh, I love you such much!" she tells the giggling little boy as she plants kisses on his tummy.

"Could you be any sweeter?" She hugs six-year-old Sage and pulls three-year-old Jemma into her lap. All the children are chattering at once, telling their mother about their day. After a few minutes, their father, Bob, a gentle bear of a man with a dark beard, herds the kids toward the kitchen. "Mommy's busy right now. Let's get a snack," he tells them. "Thanks, honey," Dawn murmurs, giving her husband's hand an affectionate squeeze.

Seeing Dawn today in such a peaceful setting, surrounded by her loving family, it is nearly impossible to imagine where she's come from. Looking at her—beautiful, strong, confident, and funny—an observer would think, "She's always had her act together." But most of Dawn's thirty-nine years of life have been anything but serene. She is the survivor of a chaotic, abusive childhood; an adolescence spent mostly on the street, and a marriage filled with savage violence.

Looking back, it seems as though Dawn was

Dawn

Dawn and her husband, Bob, share an affectionate moment.

marked for misfortune from the beginning. Her parents divorced when she was a baby. Her father went off to "do his thing" and left Dawn with her mother. Dawn's mother, a pretty twenty-one-year-old, "wasn't especially maternal," Dawn says wryly. She quickly tired of being responsible for the little girl and signed custody over to Dawn's paternal grandmother, Peggy, and Peggy's husband, Dan. Peggy and Dan moved with Dawn to Germany, where Dan was in the service.

Dawn remembers her early life with her grandparents as "pretty normal." She had started kindergarten in Germany when her mother, who had remarried, decided she wanted her six-year-old daughter back. She filed for a change of custody, which the courts granted. Dawn's grandparents reluctantly returned the child to the States.

But any hopes that Dawn had of a normal family life with her mother and stepfather were soon destroyed. Her stepfather, Larry, was a tall, strong

Sitting on the front step of their house, Dawn cuddles with her
daughter Jemma and son Sage.

man with four daughters from a previous marriage.
He also had a huge thirst for alcohol and a mean
streak a mile wide. He beat his wife, he beat his
daughters, and he beat Dawn. Soon Dawn's mother
became physically violent as well; after Larry would

hit her, she would turn her pent-up anger on her little daughter.

As the years went by, Larry's drunken rages and beatings turned into something even uglier. When Dawn's mother was out of the house, he would often drunkenly stumble into the bedroom Dawn shared with one of her stepsisters. There he would rape them, warning them that no one would believe them if they told.

Sure enough, when Dawn went to her mother for help, her mother slapped her across the face and told her never to repeat such lies again. (Incredibly, years later, she told Dawn that although she knew Larry molested his own daughter, she didn't think he would do the same to her.)

Dawn's grandparents tried to intercede. The rest of Dawn's childhood and teen years were filled with trips to family court and short-lived changes of custody. She bounced between her mother's home in Georgia and the home of her grandparents, who were now living in New Jersey. Occasionally she stayed with her father and his new wife and family in Pennsylvania, but a savage knock-down fight with her father, in which she was eventually thrown out into the snow with no coat or boots, ended that.

Nowhere felt like a safe refuge, and Dawn began going wild. Hanging out on the streets was preferable to going home; the high that drugs and alcohol provided were a welcome change from the turmoil of her life. What began to feel "normal" was staying in shelters, sharing apartments with prostitutes and drug dealers, or sleeping on friends' couches, in abandoned vehicles, and in makeshift sheds in the woods. "I felt at ease in the streets," she says today. "There, I wasn't trapped. Being homeless had its own dangers, but they were nothing compared to the dangers of living with my family."

Surprisingly, Dawn managed to stay in school, eventually earning her high school diploma. School was a place to take a shower, get something to eat,

Dawn and Bob's youngest son, Zane, gets a lift from his dad.

and see her friends. "I didn't get much of an academic education," she says, "but I did get educated. I learned that I couldn't depend on anyone. My trust in my fellow human beings was just about non-existent." The night of her high school graduation in New Jersey, her friends presented her with a bottle of blackberry brandy and a bus ticket to upstate Pennsylvania. There she crashed with some friends in a low-income housing project until the landlord caught on and threw her out. For most of the next year she was homeless, sleeping on friends' couches during the day and running the streets with drug dealers and prostitutes at night. Eventually her grandmother came looking for her, and she returned to New Jersey.

Soon after, around the time of her nineteenth birthday, a friend invited her to a keg party. She wanted Dawn to meet someone. That someone was Den, a tall, good-looking factory worker. He and Dawn hung out that evening, and soon became a couple.

What did Dawn like about Den? She smiles wryly at the question. "Oh, he was perfect," she answers sarcastically. "He'd party. He was as big a pothead as

I was a drinker."

Turning more serious, she adds, "I guess he was an escape. I felt like I was back at Square One, you know—back living with my grandparents, with absolutely no sense of any future for myself."

Dawn had always been an energetic, Type A person. "I always wanted to go, to do, to be something," she says. "I just had no idea what." Now she began working three jobs so she could afford a cheap apartment in a bad part of town. Soon Den moved in with her.

On the surface, Den's background seemed far more stable than Dawn's. He was the youngest of seven children born to an Irish Catholic farm family. By the time Dawn met him, his mother was working as a waitress, earning her own money, and she and her husband lived very separate lives within their house. But Den's sisters told Dawn that their earlier lives had been quite different. When Den's mother had been at home full-time raising her large family, her husband had frequent outbursts of anger and had hit her often. Although Den, the "baby," hadn't witnessed the beatings, Dawn later wondered how much of his father's behavior Den was imitating.

At first, living with Den was okay, by Dawn's standards. He was irritable if he'd run out of pot, or when he was hung over. He would call Dawn names, curse at her, or push her when he was in a particularly bad mood. But compared to what Dawn had lived with, these things were nothing. And getting high together was fun.

Then Den's mother became seriously ill. Although she had seven children, no one was available to help. So Dawn quit her jobs, as well as the beauty school she had begun attending, and she and Den moved in with his parents. Living in the basement of Den's family home, Dawn began to get another sense of his family. His father spoke little, but when he would come downstairs to do his laundry or Dawn would go upstairs to use the bathroom, he would mutter angrily that she and Den were sinning by living together. In response to his pressuring, the two got married.

Eventually Den's mother died, and the newly-weds bought a house together. For Dawn, having a house of her own was a dream come true. Finally, she believed, she was in a place that no one could throw her out of or take away from her. She loved the house fiercely and threw herself into decorating it, dreaming of filling it with children and finally having a happy family life.

But soon the house itself was her only source of pleasure. With every passing day, Den became more foul-tempered. "It was as if with each bit of added responsibility, he became more angry," Dawn says. "First we buried his mother. Then we bought the house. Bills came in. I was working nights. Anything out of the ordinary routine would set him off."

A favorite target was Dawn's weight. "Everything was 'you fat pig' this and 'you fat pig' that," she says.

Sage, Zane, and Jemma help their mom with some yard work.

He told her she was fat, she was ugly, and that her family was grateful to him for having taken her off their hands. When she threatened to leave, he laughed at her. "No one else will ever want a fat pig like you," he told her.

Desperate and humiliated, Dawn went through a stomach-stapling surgery in order to lose weight. During the surgery, her doctor discovered that the years of beatings from Larry and her mother had mangled her spleen. The organ needed to be removed. She healed badly from the surgery, developing pneumonia and then a blood infection. And she didn't lose weight.

"And the funny thing is," Dawn says today, "I look back at photographs of me from that time, and I was not fat."

Two years into their relationship, Den graduated from curses and pushes and name-calling to physical violence.

It was Dawn's twenty-first birthday. She wanted to go out to celebrate. Den didn't. Dawn called a girlfriend and the two drove to the Jersey shore and bar-hopped until the early morning hours. When Dawn arrived home, loud, drunk, and happy, Den was furious that she had gone out.

As she stood in her kitchen doorway talking with him, Den shoved her out of the way so he could get to the beer in the refrigerator. She objected. The two began shouting at each other. Den snapped. He landed a backhand blow to her jaw, shoved her down on the bed, and began choking her, all the time shouting vile abuse in her face. He then stormed out, going to his parents' house for the night.

The next day when he returned, Den was all remorse. In tears, he apologized. "I'm so sorry," he said. Dawn hugged him and said it was all right. "I'll never hurt you again," he promised.

"Never again," though, was soon in coming. Once Den began to hit Dawn, he seemed powerless to stop. A bad day at work; a meal served late; running out of marijuana—anything could set him off. When Dawn became pregnant, he was wild with anger. "He definitely did not want to be a father," she says. "He was really bitter about how hard his mother had had to work to raise her kids, and he took that out on me." She soon lost the baby.

After Den's first punch to Dawn's face, he avoided that area. He specialized in body shots, so

Dawn, Jemma, and Sage pile into their favorite oversized chair.

her bruises were covered by her clothing. But as their fifth year together rolled around, he crossed that line as well. During one beating, he battered her so badly that her face was deeply bruised and both eyes were blackened. In response, he went out and bought Dawn a tube of Dermablend, a special makeup created to cover bruises, scars, and birthmarks.

Dawn

"I was something he needed to disguise," Dawn says bitterly. "Just like we disguised our relationship and pretended we were a normal couple."

During all these years, Dawn's life with Den followed a predictable routine. Den got up in the morning, got high, went to the factory, got high at lunch, came home, had dinner, and got high. Dawn came home from her job at the local cable company and began drinking Jack Daniels as she prepared dinner. If Den were in a good mood, Dawn might share his marijuana. If not, he might beat her up. Eventually she'd drink herself into a stupor and pass out for the night. On weekends, the pair might have a cookout with friends with whom they'd get drunk and high, occasionally with crank (methamphetamine) as well as marijuana.

Their friends did not concern themselves with Dawn and Den's troubles. Dawn's grandparents occasionally saw her with bruises on her face and told her not to tolerate Den's beatings, so she avoided them. When she became acquainted with her half-brother (an illegitimate son of her father's) and became close friends with him, he was horrified to realize what was going on. On several occasions he contacted Den and threatened him if he didn't stop hurting Dawn. In response, Dawn says, "Den pulverized me." On one occasion, she was asleep when the brother telephoned. She was awakened by the infuriated Den's fists slamming into her. Soon he insisted that her brother never again come to their house. Like the robot she was beginning to feel like, she obeyed.

"At first, I fought back," she says, sounding weary just at the memory. "I was strong, and he was a skinny guy. But like I always say—crazy beats strong any day. Against that kind of crazy rage, I didn't have a chance."

And so she went on, day after day, "on auto pilot." She was drinking more heavily than ever, and if she allowed herself to think about the future, she assumed that she would not live much longer. Either Den would beat her to death or she would take her own life. But finally an evening came that shook her out of her stupor.

By the time Den got home from work that night, he was already drunk. Shaking her head in disgust, Dawn went on cooking dinner. He grabbed a beer out of the refrigerator and stumbled toward their bedroom. Soon she smelled the sweet odor of marijuana wafting down the hallway. Then she heard Den cursing angrily; he had spilled his pot. Dawn put dinner on the table and sat down to wait for him.

Den emerged from the bedroom and began weaving unsteadily toward the kitchen. He stumbled over his own feet and responded by furiously punching his fist through the wall. When he reached the dining table, he glared down at the plate Dawn had set for him.

"From then on," Dawn reports, "everything felt like it was happening in slow motion."

Den sent his filled plate flying into the wall, then connected a hard backhand blow to Dawn's jaw. Swallowing her own blood, she ran from the table, but he pounced on her in the hallway and threw her to the floor. Under his ceaseless rain of blows, her pain grew so intense that she lost consciousness.

When Dawn opened her eyes, she was lying on the ground in the woods behind her house. Den had dragged her there. He was still sitting on top of her, but he wasn't hitting her. Instead, she felt something cold and metallic pressing against her throat. In a moment of sickening clarity, she realized it was the barrel of her own handgun, a .357 Magnum that she had bought years ago for protection. She tried to scream, but as if she were in a nightmare, no sound came out.

CLICK! Den had pulled the trigger. But she was still alive. Then she remembered—the last time she had cleaned the gun, she had not reloaded it.

When Den realized there were no bullets in the

Sitting at the kitchen table, the family celebrates Dawn's birthday.

gun, he went mad with rage. Using the barrel of the gun as a hammer, he beat Dawn until she passed out once again.

Hours later, Dawn awakened. This time she was alone. She lay in the cold dirt sobbing until no more tears would come. Then she crawled out of the woods and to the driveway of her house, where her car was parked. She found the car key that she always kept hidden under the fender.

A glance in the window confirmed that Den had passed out on the couch and would not hear her start the car. As she pulled away from the house, she took a look at herself in the rear-view mirror. She told the bloody, bruised, swollen woman looking back at her that she would never allow anyone to hurt her again.

Over the years, Dawn had called the police for help many times. But she had always refused to press charges against Den. This time she was ready. She drove to a pay phone, called the police, and then went into the station to file charges. The next time she saw her husband was in court. She left with a hefty restraining order against him and possession of the house.

"I walked out of the courtroom feeling terrific," she remembers. "But then a victim's advocate who was working with me took my arm. She said, 'Don't take the elevator down. He's probably waiting for you there. Instead, take the back stairs.' I thought, 'But...I have a *restraining order!* Why do I have to hide from him?'" It was Dawn's first hint that legal remedies might not be enough to keep her safe.

Dawn returned to her house, relieved to be able to live in it alone. She changed the locks and hoped that Den would be intimidated enough by her pressing charges that he wouldn't bother her again.

Her hopes ended two weeks later. It was a beautiful fall afternoon and she was standing at the kitchen sink, washing dishes. She had left the front door open to let in the warm autumn air. Suddenly Den was standing in the kitchen, holding a potted plant and a pumpkin.

He sweetly said, "I know fall is your favorite time of year, so I brought you these. Let's go for a ride."

Dawn tried not to look as frightened as she felt. She knew—and Den knew—that their neighbors were all at work. No one would hear her if she screamed.

Zane enjoys a piece of his mom's birthday cake.

"I said, 'You're not supposed to be here.'" As soon as the words left her lips, Dawn saw the flash of a kitchen knife as it flew past her face. Certain she was going to die, she collapsed in a faint. When she woke up, she was alone. "I can only guess that my fainting scared him enough that he left," she says.

Whatever small sense of security Dawn had felt was gone. Den began calling her at work, threatening to kill her if she did not let him have the house. Her supervisor started taping her incoming phone calls, and she even got on the phone to let Den know that his threats were being recorded. Nothing had any effect. Dawn realized that a restraining order was not enough to protect her from someone as violent and out of control as Den.

Meanwhile, friends had begun to rally around Dawn. One was a co-worker, Bob. He was everything that was foreign to Dawn: a kind man, a college-educated man, from a loving and stable family. "I couldn't imagine what he saw in me," Dawn says now. But he liked her and he was worried sick about her. He and other friends told her, over and over, to leave her house and get Den out of her life.

For a long time, Dawn couldn't hear them. "For them, the worst thing was that Den would eventually kill me," she says. "But I was more afraid of being homeless than dying."

Finally, though, Bob said something that got through to Dawn. He told her, "That is not a home. That is just a house. You can get another house. But you can't get another life."

Dawn realized he was right. But by then, she was utterly exhausted, demoralized, and generally beaten down. In her words, "I was a zombie—just completely out of gas." She told her friends to do what they thought was best. They quickly found her an apartment, cleared out the house, and moved her belongings into her new place.

During the whole process, Dawn was numb. "I remember the afternoon they were carrying my stuff into the apartment," she says. "I was sitting on the tailgate of the truck, looking at them. One of them was an old friend from way back. He was a typical

New Jersey 'piney,' covered with tattoos, with blond hair down to his waist. The other was Bob, this college graduate from a good home. It was as though I was seeing a vision of my past and my future."

As she sat on that tailgate, she saw kids riding their bikes and heard neighbors greeting each other. She felt enormously out of place. "It was total Norman Rockwell suburbia, and it freaked me out. All I could think about was, 'Where's the liquor store?'" As soon as her friends left, she went in search of it, even talking the owner into taking her out-of-town check for a giant bottle of Jack Daniels.

Leaving the house had its intended effect; Den stopped threatening her. But merely being away from her abuser did not heal Dawn. Like the survivor of a war, she was suffering from post-traumatic stress. She continued to drink heavily. Her sleep was interrupted by nightmares of Den coming for her with a gun. She imagined that when the houseplant hanging in the window swayed in the night breeze, it was

When Dawn looks at her happy little girl, she sometimes thinks
how different their childhoods have been.

Den reaching out to grab her. Doctors gave her
sleeping pills and antidepressants, "but they just
whacked me out."

Throughout this dark time, Bob was a constant,

patient presence. He would sit by her bed at night, rubbing her head and talking soothingly to her, not leaving until she fell asleep. In the morning, she would find a note from him, promising to call her later in the day. "And he always did," she says.

Dawn found a therapist that she trusted and worked hard on regaining a sense of optimism and trust. Slowly the terrifying visions faded, and Dawn felt herself returning to life. Her divorce from Den became final in 1991; about a year later, Bob asked her to marry him. Deeply in love, she accepted. Together, the couple bought a house—this time, a place that would be a true home for them both. They joyfully planned to fill it with children.

But Dawn soon learned that having a good husband and a safe home did not mean life would be stress-free. Pregnancy did not occur; doctors said Dawn might never be able to have children. Then she miscarried. All her old demons resurfaced, telling her, "You're worthless; you're a loser." She turned to her old comforter: alcohol. "I drank myself into oblivion," she confesses. "I'd come home from work, pull down the shades, and drink. It was a terrible time in our marriage." Realizing how close she was to losing everything she loved, she called her therapist and began seeing her again, sometimes with Bob. "We worked it through," she reports. "But without the help of someone from outside, who could talk objectively to us both, I don't know if we would have made it." Dawn began attending Alcoholics Anonymous meetings. She's been "clean and sober" for nine years.

She and Bob decided to adopt. But shortly before their first appointment with an adoption agency, she became pregnant with their oldest child, Sage. Two years later, along came Jemma, and in another two years a second son, Zane, joined the family.

Today Dawn, her husband and kids, the cat and the dog are all living in what looks a lot like the "Norman Rockwell suburbia" that once scared and

Dawn washes chocolate frosting off Zane's hand. Making her
children feel safe and loved is a top priority.

Now a strong, healthy woman, Dawn has experienced abuse, addiction, and homelessness.

confused her so. There's even a white picket fence around the house. But Dawn never forgets where she came from. And she has dedicated herself to helping others who might be trapped in similar nightmares. Dawn is now employed as a case manager for a soup kitchen in Camden, New Jersey. She attends college and is working on her certificate in addictions counseling, and hopes to eventually earn a master's degree and practice as a clinical therapist.

But dearest to her heart is the organization she has founded, Healing Mama. (The website is **www.healingmama.org.**) Its purpose is to support mothers who are recovering from addiction. "I started Healing Mama because as a mother myself, I realized that there's nothing like a screaming baby at 3 a.m. to make you want to dive into that bottle," she explains. "But that wasn't an option for me, so when the kids were smaller I began looking around for support. There were mothers' groups in our area, but when I went to their meetings, I felt so out of the loop. Those women's concerns weren't like mine."

Dawn sent out an e-mail to the mailing lists of a couple of mom's organizations she knew about. In it, she asked if there were other women interested in a group focusing specifically on the concerns of moms recovering from addiction while trying to "keep it together" for their families. To her astonishment, she received hundreds of responses, some from as far away as Australia. Using letters and essays from some of those women, as well as her own writing, Dawn put together the first six-page Healing Mama newsletter. Since then she has produced eleven issues of the newsletter, which has grown to fourteen pages. Some are sent out to subscribers, but most Dawn gives away when she does public speaking about her experience as a battered, addicted woman.

Sitting today in the warmth of her comfortable home, surrounded by the people who love her, Dawn struggles to find words to describe her feelings about where her life's journey has brought her.

Dawn

Gesturing toward her laughing children and smiling husband, this once homeless, addicted, beaten woman finally says, "Having all this—I am living a life beyond all my dreams."

Ryan

Ryan Klootwyk

"**W**hen you talk to kids at school about me, tell them my name is Larry Taylor. Got that? Larry *Taylor*. Never use my real name."

Seven-year-old Ryan Klootwyk nodded. His new stepfather's last name wasn't Taylor. Ryan didn't know why Larry wanted to use a false name. But one thing he did know was that you didn't question Larry. You just did what he said, and otherwise stayed out of his way. That way nobody would get hurt. Maybe.

When Ryan's mother became pregnant with him, she and her husband were living in Germany. Ryan's father had been serving in the military there. Both Ryan's parents were very young, just nineteen, and they already had a one-year-old son, Frank Jr. Shortly before Ryan's birth, they returned to their home-town of Muskegon, a city in western Michigan.

The marriage lasted until Ryan was four. "Dad was a hound dog," Ryan says, matter-of-factly. "He didn't want to settle down with just one woman." Frank Sr. also began getting involved in drugs, not only using them, but selling them. Before long, he had established himself as one of the major drug deal-ers in the area. "Psychedelic Frank," as he was known, was the guy to go to if you wanted to get high.

As a little boy, Ryan didn't understand that his dad was a heroin addict or a drug dealer. He did notice that when Frank Sr. showed up to see his sons, he was often driving a new car. On one occasion, he pulled up in a shiny black and silver hearse. "He took us to McDonald's in it," Ryan says. "I still remem-ber how people stared." And he remembers his dad's house as "hippie heaven—all black light posters, shag rugs, fringed leather, and a very young girlfriend."

Ryan

Ryan shares a laugh with his sons, Ryan Jr. and Reid.

"I don't have many in-depth memories of my dad," Ryan says. "It's more like snapshots. For instance, I remember him walking into the house once while we were watching *The Wizard of Oz* and giving me a dollar. I remember going out to get ice cream with him. He was a bubbly guy, fun. But as far as being a father, there was nothing solid there. It always seemed like there was something more important to him than being with us."

85

Since their divorce, Frank Sr. and Ryan's mom had remained friends—"almost like brother and sister," Ryan recalls. Frank Sr. seemed protective of his ex-wife, running off boyfriends that he thought didn't treat her well. There were a lot of noisy parties; Ryan and Frank Jr. were often left with their mother's young girlfriends for long periods. On the weekends, Ryan's grandfather would sometimes stop in and be outraged by what he'd find. "He'd dump sleeping people off the couch, kick them out of the house, and roar at my mom about the 'damn hippies' and how she was hanging out with the wrong people."

When Larry came on the scene, Frank Sr. was not happy. "He was acquainted with Larry," Ryan says. "He tried to warn Mom that Larry was bad news, but she didn't pay attention." And looking back, Ryan can understand why she didn't, at first.

"When you first met Larry, there was nothing not to like," he remembers. "He was a charmer. Extremely likeable. Extremely smooth. Extremely handsome. To this day, it's a little hard for me to see a Clint Eastwood movie, because Larry could be the guy's brother."

Larry was also a savage psychopath, as terrifying as any movie villain. But that didn't become apparent right away.

He not only romanced Ryan's mother; he charmed the whole family. He took the boys fishing and encouraged them to call him "Dad." He bought new furniture for the house. Everything seemed great.

Then one day, a car pulled up in the yard. Ryan's cousin bolted out of it, screaming and crying. She ran into the house, gasping, "Frank's dead! Frank's dead!"

"My mom freaked out, completely lost her mind," Ryan recalls. "She pulled the screen door off the hinges and started breaking things. I was terrified."

Eventually he learned what had happened: Frank Sr. had been found dead in his home, a bullet wound to his head. The death was ruled a suicide. "And he may well have killed himself," Ryan says. "But a lot

Family activities, such as playing board games, are important to Ryan, Ronda, and their sons.

of people still believe that he owed too much money to the wrong people and that they killed him. In any case, I don't think the police went out of their way to figure out what had happened. He'd been a major headache to them, and he was gone."

Six-year-old Ryan was numb with grief and confusion. "I couldn't really comprehend what had happened," he says. "All I knew was that this guy, who I was always hoping might be around more, had disappeared forever."

In Frank Sr.'s absence, Larry made his move. "My mom had been kind of a mess already, and now she was just crushed, completely vulnerable," he says. "Larry told her what she wanted to hear. They began using heroin together. In no time at all, he was living in our house."

Some months later, the terrifying side of Larry made its first appearance.

The kids had a dog which had originally belonged to Frank Sr. One evening, it had an accident on the carpet. Larry, who was drunk as well as high, threatened to kill the animal. Eight-year-old Frank Jr. objected. "Don't hurt the dog! That's my dad's dog!" he cried.

Larry ignored the little boy, but then Ryan's mother overheard the commotion and walked in. "Larry, what are you doing?" she asked.

"It was like somebody threw a switch," Ryan

remembers. In a second's time, Larry's face changed, turning from merely irritated to cold, hard, and murderous. Without a word, he punched her in the face with his closed fist. Terrified, the little boys hid behind a table and watched as he struck her again and again.

Finally, Larry stopped hitting, and Ryan's mom and the children fled to the boys' bedroom. Larry followed and cornered the boys. Putting his face close to theirs, he hissed out an order. "Don't you ever, ever mention your father to me again."

In the hours, then days that followed, Ryan and Frank waited for their mother's response to Larry's violence. Would she kick Larry out? Would they move away? Would she call the police? But nothing happened. Her face still swollen and bruised from the beating, their mother told them Larry was sorry. He had apologized. He felt very bad about what had happened. It wouldn't happen again.

But it did happen again, and again, and again. It

A bike ride gives the Klootwyks some time for family togetherness.

became routine for the boys to spend nights huddling in their bedroom, pillows over their heads, listening to Larry shouting, their mom screaming, and the sounds of blows. "I couldn't begin to tell you how often there were scenes like that," says Ryan today. "I could write a book the length of *War and Peace* about them. Only there would be a lot more 'war' than 'peace.'

"Larry was, without a doubt, the most unpredictable human being I've ever met," Ryan continues. "He could go from laughing to totally enraged, or from angry to smiling, in the blink of an eye. No one ever knew what would set him off. There was no rule book."

A sad example of Larry's unpredictability involved yet another animal. The boys had been asking for a cat. Larry had said absolutely not. "A damn cat will only climb the curtains and pee on the floor," he said, using the crudest language possible. "It'll make the house stink. Besides, I just bought this couch and I don't want no worthless cat scratching it!"

And yet, one autumn day as Ryan and Frank were watching *Gilligan's Island* after school, Larry and their mom arrived home with a surprise. They were laughing and talking, obviously in good moods. When the boys heard a little voice meowing, they were overjoyed. Larry unzipped his jacket to reveal a tiny Siamese kitten.

"Can I see him? Can I hold him?" both boys exclaimed.

Larry knelt on the living room floor, kindly and gentle for once. "Just take it easy," he said, carefully placing the tiny creature on the rug. The boys watched with breathless excitement as the kitten explored its new surroundings. Then, not more than two minutes after its arrival, the cat committed an unforgivable offense. Gathering itself into an energetic little ball, it dashed across the room and clawed its way up the side of Larry's prized dark-brown velvet couch.

"GET THE HELL OFF OF MY COUCH!" Larry bellowed, swatting the cat so viciously that it did a somersault across the floor. Letting out a pathetic squeak like a child's squeeze toy, it ran to hide behind a cabinet.

Larry was wild with anger. Screaming obscenities and threats, he raged through the house. The boys knew that pleading for the kitten would only make things worse. Their mother was speaking gently to Larry, trying to calm him, as the boys vanished silently to their room.

In the morning, Ryan and Frank rushed to the kitchen, hoping desperately to find the cat. Instead they found their mother. She wasn't usually up at that hour, but today she was waiting for them.

At first she told them that the cat had run away. But faced with the boys' disbelief, she told them the truth. Larry had taken it into the back yard and killed it with a brick.

"Life was very cheap to Larry," Ryan concluded. As the violence continued, Ryan learned more about his new stepfather. He learned, for example, why he used a false last name. Larry, who liked to brag that he had spent more than half his life behind bars, was an escapee from a Georgia prison. He had been doing time there for killing two people. In addition to using a false name, Larry did what he could to change his appearance. Ryan remembers watching as

When Ryan was a boy, the idea of playing ball with his father was only a dream. He makes time for such activities with his boys.

his stepfather used sandpaper to grind away the large tattoos on both forearms.

Larry worked occasionally as a well-digger or in a body shop. But generally he supported himself by robbing houses. On one occasion, Ryan got up in the morning to find the house crammed with merchandise. There were fur coats, televisions, stereo systems, artwork, furniture—the entire contents of a wealthy family's house. Another time, when the family was living in Long Beach, California, Larry and the family were walking down a city street when Larry insisted on entering a particular jewelry store. In the store was a case of items made from ivory—"very distinctive, unusual necklaces and bracelets and figurines," Ryan says. A few days later, the entire collection showed up in the family's kitchen. Larry made a quick trip back to Muskegon, where he set up a booth selling ivory at the town's annual Art Fair.

Not surprisingly, the family moved frequently in order to keep Larry a jump ahead of the law. The moves would often occur with no notice at all. "I'd come home from school, and we'd be out the door," Ryan says. The family lived in motels and homeless shelters; in apartments and with friends. In the nearly six years that Larry was part of his life, Ryan lived in six different states and passed through fifteen schools.

Ryan's mother and brother were the only constants in his life. "They were the only ones who knew how bad things were," he remembers. "My biggest fear as a child was that I would lose them, that I would be totally alone."

When Ryan was eight, that fear nearly came true. In general, Larry's worst violence was reserved for Ryan's mother. "Larry beat Mom with reckless abandon at every opportunity," he says. "Frank and I were mostly bystanders. As long as we stayed clear and cowered in the corner and cried, he'd generally leave us out of it. He'd just beat the hell out of Mom."

That isn't to say that Larry didn't hit the boys frequently—he just didn't beat them as viciously as he did their mother.

"Larry's idea of 'discipline' was to whip us on our naked butts with the bristle side of a hairbrush until he drew blood," says Ryan. "And for a murdering wife-abuser, he was very big on table manners. Once he hauled off and cracked me against the side of my head so hard my ear rang. He said I was holding my fork the wrong way."

But one night, Ryan's brother Frank broke Larry's rules. He tried to stand up for his mother. He almost paid for it with his life.

Frank was nine. The family was living in California. Ryan can't remember what Larry was angry about that night. The reason was never very important. He began beating Ryan's mom even more savagely than usual. When she fell down on the floor and curled into a ball, trying to protect her face and head, he started stomping her. As usual, he was wearing his prized, heavy-soled black motorcycle boots.

Frank couldn't take it. He threw his small body between Larry and his mother and shouted, "Leave her alone! Don't hit her!" Instantly, Larry turned on the nine-year-old and landed a flying kick to the child's face.

When Larry was done, Frank was semi-conscious. One eye was swollen shut, pus and fluid oozing out of it. Back in their bedroom, little Ryan spent the night watching over his wounded brother. "Nothing

Larry ever did hurt me inside more than when he hurt my brother like that."

In the morning Frank seemed a little better, and his mother took him to the hospital. Ryan went along. Before they left, Larry coached them in what they should say. "Tell them you were playing baseball and Frank got hit in the face with the bat," Larry said. Both boys and their mother obediently lied. Still, the injury made people at the hospital suspicious. A police officer took the children aside and asked them what had really happened. They stuck to Larry's story.

"I wanted to tell the truth, but we were so afraid of Larry," says Ryan. "We knew what would happen if we told the truth. They would take him away, he would be in jail for a short time, and then he would come out and get us and kill Mom."

Without the boys' cooperation, the police could do nothing. And a few weeks later, Larry, aware of the watchful eye of the police, decided to move the

Reid shares a moment with the family parrot.

family again. In yet another state and another school, the violence continued.

Amazingly, throughout this hellish period of his life, Ryan did well in school. In third grade, he won a school reading contest. The prize was a copy of *Charlotte's Web*. The story about the little runt pig and the kind, clever spider who saved his life became a favorite. The crazier his home life became, the more he turned to books as a refuge. "Reading was a way I could forget about everything," he says. "It was the only thing that was completely in my control. I am not sure if I would have survived without it." He looked for things to read the way a hungry child might look for food. "Once I even found some old history textbooks in the school trash can. To someone, those old books were trash, but to me they were a treasure. I took them home and read them cover to cover."

Ryan's success at school had no effect on his troubled home life. As he moved from one new school to another, he hid the painful truth of his home, of his mother's addiction to heroin, and of Larry. All his teachers saw was a good student who, outwardly, seemed to be doing well. Inwardly, though, he was screaming for help.

"Sitting in all those classrooms, I remember thinking, 'Why doesn't anybody do something?'" Ryan remembers. "I desperately wanted someone to ask about us, to investigate, to care. But I was incapable of asking for help. I was ashamed about what was happening to us, ashamed at what Mom allowed to go on, ashamed that I couldn't do anything about it. And, on top of all that, I was afraid that if someone found out about our family, they might separate my mother and brother and me. I was so scared, I just kept it all inside."

He clung to the hope that someday, his mother would find the strength to leave Larry. And when he was ten, that hope was briefly realized. His mother took the two boys and fled to Michigan, not letting Larry know where they were going. For three months, Ryan was free of the constant threat of violence.

But then he returned from school one afternoon to find Larry sitting on the couch. A hateful smile lit Larry's face. "Hi," he said triumphantly. Ryan was speechless with fear.

The cycle of terror began all over again. But by now, Ryan's mother had had enough. She sought legal help and a judge granted her a restraining order that barred Larry from coming near her home. In response, Larry began stalking the family. Lying in bed one night soon after the order had been issued, Ryan heard a window break. When he went to investigate, he found Larry punching his mother. She managed to call the police, but Larry ran away before they arrived.

For three more years the family hid from Larry, moving from town to town and from school to school. Larry's stalking continued until Ryan's mother became involved with a new boyfriend. The two men got into a fight in the street and Larry was almost killed. At last, he disappeared from Ryan's life for good. (At one point, however, two FBI agents came to Ryan's house to ask if he'd seen Larry recently. He was wanted for questioning in a double murder in Oklahoma City.)

The relief of being free from Larry's violence was overwhelming. For a brief time, at age thirteen,

Ryan believed that everything was going to be all right. His mother was drug-free and had been for several years. The family was living in its own apartment, rather than staying with friends. For the first time in his life, Ryan was able to attend the same school for more than a year. He began to put down roots and make friends.

And then his mother announced that she could no longer afford the apartment they were living in. They were going to move again.

After all the years of dealing with Larry—of being the "good son," of causing no problems, of keeping his feelings bottled up—Ryan exploded. He went into ninth grade a very different person than he'd been before.

"Something inside me just snapped," he says. "I was tired of being a puppet in my mom's life. I was going to think about *me*. I was going to take charge of my life. And I thought taking charge meant rebelling. I was going to get high and goof off with my buddies and I didn't give a damn what anybody thought."

"Anybody" most definitely included his mother. Now that they were safe from Larry, Ryan began to let himself feel the anger that had built up against her. "When I was a little kid, I thought of her only as a fellow victim," he says. But looking back from a teenager's point of view, he became more resentful about her actions—or lack of action—during the Larry years. "We left, time and time again," he remembers. "We'd go to a friend's house, or to my grandparents. And then we'd go back to Larry. Frank and I would be crying, begging her not to return. She'd say, 'It'll be OK this time, guys. You'll see. He's promised to be a better person.'"

Why his mother kept returning is a question that Ryan has never satisfactorily answered to himself. "Only one person knows—and I don't really think she does, either," he says. "But she was clearly a very vulnerable person, without a great sense of self-worth.

Her marriage hadn't worked out, and I think when Dad died that really crushed her. Then Larry popped up in the midst of all that turmoil, and her defenses just collapsed. I don't think she thought she had much to live for."

Ryan was a very angry, self-destructive young man through much of his teen years. Though he was earning D's and F's in school, he clung to reading as his lifeline. "I'd skip school constantly," he remembers, "but when I did, I'd go to the public library and read." He developed a passion for stories about military history, and he particularly loved accounts of prisoners of war and how they survived. He thought of himself as a prisoner of sorts, too, locked in a jail of anger, resentment, and bad memories.

Slowly and painfully, Ryan pulled himself out of that jail. One positive step occurred when he was sixteen and met his future wife, Ronda. Like him, she had been raised by a struggling single mother, but her home had been free of fear and violence. Gradually he began to confide in her. "I was one angry jackass at the time, no question about it," Ryan says. "But soon Ronda became the person I knew I could trust. And I was smart enough to realize that she was a good influence on me. She was a good student, focused, steady. I really needed those qualities in my life."

After finishing high school, Ryan went to work as an industrial painter. The manual labor he did all day contrasted painfully with the challenging reading he did in the evenings, making his job seem boring and frustrating. Then he broke his wrist at work and had to stay home for a while. By that time, he and Ronda were married and expecting their first child. He looked ahead at his future, and he did not like what he saw.

"I became aware of how I had hurt myself by wasting time and making poor choices," Ryan says. Deciding not to waste any more time, he enrolled in community college. To his surprise and delight, he found that his long-buried academic abilities were still alive, although a little rusty. Eventually he was a solid A student. Upon finishing community college, he enrolled in a university, where he earned a degree in history and secondary education. He is now working as a substitute high school teacher while he waits for a full-time position to open in his area.

But far more important than his schooling and career is Ryan's family. He and Ronda are the parents of two happy, confident young boys: Reid, eleven, and Ryan Jr., thirteen. Looking at his two sons, Ryan Sr. frequently thinks of the contrast between their childhoods and those of him and his brother. Their lives could not be much more different.

"They say that children who were abused grow up to be abusers, and I guess that is often true," Ryan says. "But even with all the violence around me, I somehow developed a strong sense of the family I wanted some day. When I got a chance to be a father, I swore I was going to do whatever it took. I would never let my wife or children go through what

Ryan met his wife, Ronda, when both were in high school. In contrast to his chaotic behavior, Ronda was "steady and focused."

we went through.

"That doesn't mean that I am never angry!" he says, adding jokingly, "Do I ever want to strangle my wife? Do I ever want to throw the boys over the moon?" He laughs at his own exaggeration. "Sure, I get mad, and so does Ronda, and so do the boys. But no matter what, there is not and will never be any violence in this house. I made myself a promise long ago: My kids will have a father they are not afraid of. My kids will never need to be afraid for their mom. I have defined myself that way, I guess. Maybe that's not much. But to me, it's the best definition of a husband and father there is."

Eunice

Eunice Ruiz

One hot afternoon in 1998, Eunice Ruiz and her mother were riding the subway in Mexico City. They were arguing, as they often did. Eunice was in her mid-twenties, a special education teacher living in Texas. Her mother was pushing her to move permanently back to Mexico. As always, Eunice said no; she would rather stay in Texas. Her mother became more upset. Eunice became more frustrated.

"I had not planned to say anything special to her that day," Eunice said. "But suddenly I heard my voice saying, 'Let me tell you what happened to me when I was a child in Mexico.'"

Eunice was the oldest of three sisters. Their father was a minister and their mother a housewife. They lived in a comfortable house in Mexico City.

In addition to working as a classroom teacher, Eunice tutors
students like this boy during the summer.

Life was "just normal; regular," Eunice remembers. She loved her mom, but she was especially close
to her dad, who enjoyed and encouraged Eunice's
sharp intelligence. "Dad spent a great deal of time
with me, always teaching me something," she says.
"He taught me to read music and play the piano.
When he couldn't teach me any more, he found a
tutor for me. He encouraged me to read and write and

learn about current events. Dad was happy that I was a 'book person.' On the other hand, I think my mother would have preferred if I'd spent more time learning to cook and do 'girl' things around the house." Growing up, she learned to crave both parents' approval. "I never, ever wanted to disappoint them."

Like many Mexican families, the Ruizes lived surrounded by their extended family. Many neighboring houses were occupied by Eunice's aunts, uncles, and cousins. Family gatherings were large, frequent, and fun.

It was at such a gathering that Eunice's ordinary little-girl life ended. Everyone was at the home of some cousins who were in the business of upholstering furniture. One room was filled with big pieces of foam, the kind used to make cushions for couches and chairs. Eight-year-old Eunice and her cousins were jumping on top of the foam pieces, bouncing on them as if they were trampolines.

The children were not alone. A man was sitting

nearby, watching them. He was married to a cousin of Eunice's father. He was in his mid-thirties. His own kids were part of the gang of children playing.

That day, he called Eunice away from the other children. He began to praise and flatter her. "He told me my dad had been telling him what a smart girl I was and how well I could read," Eunice says. "He told me he needed some help."

He asked her to come into another room where it was quieter. Although the man was not a minister himself, he was active in his church, and he was planning a sermon. He handed Eunice the notes for his sermon. He asked her to read them and tell him how she thought they sounded.

Eunice obediently began to read the notes. As she read, the man approached her from behind. He pulled her pants down, opened his own pants, and pressed himself against her. Shocked and confused, Eunice did and said nothing. When the man was done, he pulled her pants back up and set her on his

Reading has always been one of Eunice's favorite hobbies.

lap. Then he asked her what she had thought of the sermon.

Eunice left the room in a daze. It was soon time to go home. She climbed silently into her parents' car and rode home wordlessly. In the familiar, safe environment of her parents' house, she tried not to think about what had just happened.

"I had no idea what he had done, or why," she

says. "I knew nothing about sex, nothing at all. All I knew was that my mother had told me never to touch myself 'down there.' She said it was wrong. And now I had let someone else touch me there. I felt dirty, and scared, and as if I had done something terribly bad."

The cousin's husband continued to victimize Eunice. "It was always a similar situation," she says. "There would be a lot of kids running around and playing, and no one would notice if one disappeared for a bit." Feeling powerless to tell anyone, Eunice protected herself the only way she could think of. At the family gatherings, she attached herself tightly to her mother's side, never leaving to play with the other children. Eventually the man seemed to lose interest in her. Years later, she would find out why.

Pushing aside thoughts of her molestation, Eunice concentrated on being a "good girl" and disappointing no one. She did exceptionally well in school, earning straight A's. She practiced piano dili-

As a child, Eunice dreamed of being a concert pianist.
Now she plays just for fun.

gently, even dreaming of a career as a concert pianist.

Then, when she was thirteen, a terrible thing happened. Eunice's father, who she had loved and

Eunice prepares notes for a meeting of the youth group she helps
lead at her church.

admired so much, died of cancer.

"I was devastated," she says. Her ability to con-
centrate on schoolwork vanished. Her straight A's
plummeted, eventually becoming D's and F's.

Not long after her dad's death, some family
friends visited Mrs. Ruiz. They mentioned that their
son was applying to Presbyterian Pan-American
School in Kingsville, Texas. This mission school was

one where many Mexican clergy sent their children to learn English as well as get a high school education. Mrs. Ruiz thought that it might be good for Eunice to attend Pan-American. She could learn English, and the change of scene might do her good.

Eunice received a scholarship and began school in Texas. She gradually became fluent in English and began to do well again academically. But as time went on, she became more aware that something was very wrong.

"I felt like a freak," she says. "I never felt that I fit in. I was constantly afraid I would do or say the wrong thing." She had friends, but she had no faith that their friendship would last. "If people seemed to like me, I was sure it was only because they couldn't see what a bad person I was on the inside. I was haunted by my past and the bad thing I thought that I had done."

As she grew older, she saw friends dating, flirting, and having fun with boys. She froze inside at the thought. "I had friends who were boys, including one I considered my best friend. But I was terrified to be alone even with him. I would think, 'OK, when are you going to hurt me?' I was sure it was just a matter of time before it happened."

"I just didn't like myself, my physical self," she continues. "I never enjoyed being a girl. To this day, sexuality is a very difficult topic for me. I automatically think of it as something dirty. I know better, but that is something that is terribly hard to overcome."

Eunice stayed on at Pan-American until she graduated. She then enrolled at Texas A&M University, earned a bachelor's degree, and began working as a special education teacher in Raymondville, Texas. She liked her job, but her personal life was becoming more and more painful. She was deeply depressed, spending much of her time alone and in tears. She felt trapped and desperate, without knowing quite why.

Then a friend got a job in Denton, Texas. Going with him to visit the city, she attended church there.

Eunice enjoys a visit from a friend and her baby.

As she and her friend chatted with congregation members, someone joked that she, too, should get a job in Denton. Another person chimed in, saying she knew of a special education position that was opening at the local school. Eunice called the school and was invited to interview the following Monday morning. On Monday evening, she was informed she'd gotten the job.

Moving to a new town and starting a new job filled Eunice with a sense of hope—briefly. But she soon realized that all her depression and fears had moved to Denton with her. No matter how nice her new colleagues or the people at her new church seemed, she was convinced that they would despise her if they knew the real Eunice.

Life changes come in many forms. Sometimes they are in the shape of a new person who enters our lives. Sometimes a change is sparked by a book we read, a movie we see, or a conversation we have.

The change in Eunice's life came in the form of a traffic ticket.

Around Christmas, she was cited for a traffic offense that she didn't think she'd committed. She went to court to argue against it. The judge wouldn't completely excuse her, but he offered her the chance to do some community service rather than pay a fine.

At her home computer, Eunice works on a lesson plan for school.

At the time, the local organization called "Friends of the Family" needed volunteers. As Eunice soon learned, Friends of the Family was a rape-crisis center. The center was looking for people to visit rape victims in the hospital and help them deal with what

During hard times in her life, music has always been a source
of comfort for Eunice.

had happened to them.

"The coordinator who I talked to told me all this, then said, 'Do you know anything about sexual abuse or rape?' I said, (here Eunice imitated her own very casual tone of voice) 'Oh, something like that happened to me when I was a kid, but I'm OK now.'"

"But the coordinator wasn't fooled," Eunice says. "She told me, 'Well, OK. We'd really like to have you volunteer with us, especially since you're bilingual. You'll need to start out with some training. And remember, if there's ever anything *you* want to talk about, our counseling services are free and confidential.'"

Eunice began going to her volunteer training sessions. "They taught us how to talk to rape victims," she says. "They talked about the dynamics of child sexual abuse; about the cycle of fear and guilt and depression; about what is stolen away from a rape victim. I sat there thinking, 'Dear God, this is *me*.' It was like enrolling in a class at school and realizing you already know all the answers." At the last training session, Eunice broke down crying in class. "I faced what had happened to me all those years ago," she says. "I went into counseling, and I continued with it for seven months. It was the best thing I've ever done for myself."

Meanwhile, what was happening back in Mexico?

When she heard Eunice's story, Mrs. Ruiz had burst into tears. "Where was I? Why didn't I know what had happened?" she kept asking. Eunice told her that she had been afraid to tell, had been afraid she wouldn't be believed. Then Mrs. Ruiz told Eunice something shocking.

"When she had been a little girl, my mom had been molested by an adult relative too," Eunice says. "Only when she told her mother—*her mother*—blamed my mom. She told her that she was ruined; that no man was ever going to want to marry a girl who wasn't a virgin."

But, Mrs. Ruiz added, that hadn't been true. "Mom told me that when she met my dad, she had told him what happened," Eunice said. "My dad told her it wasn't her fault, and that he loved her anyway."

"If you had told us, we would have believed you," Mrs. Ruiz assured Eunice. "And your dad would have stood up for you."

Hearing that her beloved father would have protected her was a bittersweet relief to Eunice. But she soon learned that her other fears about telling had been well-founded.

Two years after Eunice's conversation with her mother, a fifteen-year-old cousin in Mexico City tried to commit suicide. At the hospital, she told the people caring for her that she wanted to die to get away from a man who was molesting her—the same man who had molested Eunice.

When Mrs. Ruiz heard this story from the girl's mother, she said, "It's true. He did the same thing to my daughter."

The story spread through the extended family like wildfire. Other girls reported that they, too, had been victimized by the same man. Soon, a group of family members confronted him. At first he denied everything. But when they brought up the name of Eunice, whose father had been a highly respected member of the family, he admitted what he had done. He and his family then moved away to another part of Mexico.

It was at this point that Eunice began to see just how painful and negative the response to a sexual abuse victim can be, even if she is believed.

"I was away in Texas, so it didn't affect me as much," she says. "But people were very angry at my cousin, the one who had tried to kill herself. The message seemed to be, 'OK, we're sorry this happened to you, but how dare you make us deal with it! You've split up the family!'" To this day, Eunice says, when the family gets together, small children will come up to the cousin and say, "It's your fault that (the molester's name) isn't here. You made him go away."

Sexual abuse is hard to deal with in any culture, but Eunice thinks that it presents some special obstacles for Hispanic families.

"My dad's family—the side of the family that this man came from—is very stereotypical," she says.

"Machismo is powerful. The men are the bosses, and the women stay home and take care of the home and the children. Because the men are the providers, they make all the rules and decisions. Women and children are not supposed to question them. So if you say out loud that a man has done something wrong, that shakes the whole structure of the society.

"Also," Eunice continues, "there's a strong sense in our culture that a 'good girl' behaves a certain way. It's your responsibility to make sure that men don't get 'ideas' about you. So if a man does hurt you, it's because you put bad thoughts in his head, and it's your fault." She adds bitterly, "Even if you're eight."

As Eunice has become more outspoken about her own story, the horror and the fears that haunted her have gradually faded away. Recently she has become a volunteer with the Texas Association Against Sexual Abuse (TAASA), and she speaks about her experience before school groups and other community organizations. As she speaks, she thinks of the girls and

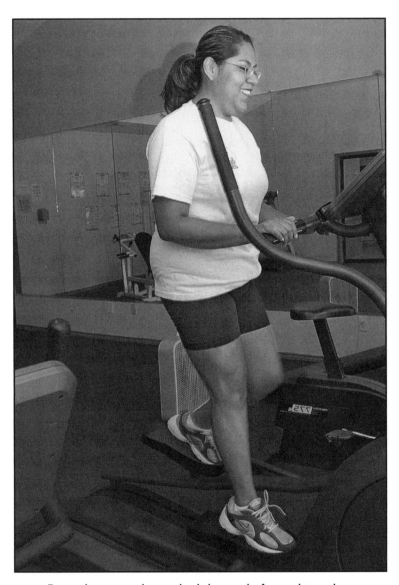

Eunice has recently reached the goal of completing her
first marathon.

women who are sitting there hiding their own secret of sexual abuse, too ashamed to speak it aloud.

"When something awful happens to you and you keep it buried inside, it's easy to start believing that your story is the worst, that you are uniquely dirty and horrible, and that no one would ever, ever be able to accept you if they knew the truth about you," Eunice says. "I felt that way. I let being molested define who I was."

Today, she says, things are different. "I have spoken out about what happened to me. I have put the responsibility where it belongs—on the man who hurt me. I have learned to accept myself and to see the good things that make me what I am. My scars are still there, but they are only scars. They are no longer open wounds."

A Special Offer

If you enjoyed this book, Townsend Press
has a special offer for you.
Turn the page to learn how to obtain five
entertaining, readable books
free of charge
except for shipping and handling.

Why Become a Regular Reader?

Many people believe that reading is the very heart of education. Here is what they say:

1. Reading provides language power. Research has shown beyond question that frequent reading improves vocabulary, spelling, grammar, writing style, and reading speed and comprehension. If you become a regular reader, all of these language and thinking abilities develop almost automatically!

2. Reading increases the chances for job success. In today's world more than ever, jobs involve processing information, with words being the tools of the trade. Studies have found that the better your command of words, the more success you are likely to experience. *Nothing gives you a command of words like regular reading.*

3. Reading creates human power. Reading enlarges the mind and the heart. It frees us from the narrow confines of our own experience. Knowing how other people view important matters helps us decide what we ourselves think and feel. Reading also helps us connect with others and realize our shared humanity. Someone once wrote, "We read in order to know that we are not alone." We become less isolated as we share the common experiences, emotions, and thoughts that make us human. We grow more sympathetic and kind because we realize that others are like us.

And for many people, reading is a source of real enjoyment, opening the door to a lifetime of pleasure and adventure. By taking the time to walk through that door, you too may find that one of the great experiences of life is the joy of reading for its own sake.

Regular reading can, in short, change your life. The more you read, the more you know. The more you know, the more you grow.

A Special Offer

To promote your reading growth, Townsend Press will send you the following five books, edited for today's readers, at no charge except for shipping and handling.

Reading Changed
My Life!

Letters My Mother
Never Read

The Story of Blima:
A Holocaust Survivor

Jane Eyre

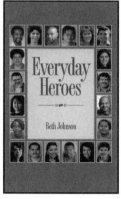

Everyday Heroes

Use the order form on the next page. Enclose five dollars to cover the cost of shipping and handling.

A Special Offer

Letters My Mother
Never Read

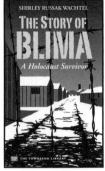

The Story of Blima:
A Holocaust Survivor

Jane Eyre

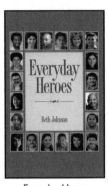

Everyday Heroes

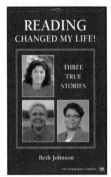

Reading Changed
My Life!

To learn more about these books and other books in the
Townsend Library, visit our website at **www.townsendpress.com**

Order Form

YES! Please send me copies of the five books shown.
Enclosed is five dollars to cover the shipping and handling.

Please PRINT very clearly. This will be your shipping label.

NAME _____

ADDRESS _____

CITY _____ STATE _____ ZIP _____

MAIL TO: TP Book Center
1038 Industrial Drive
West Berlin, NJ 08091